WHAT KIND OF SPORTS PRO ARE YOU?

By Brooke Rowe

Published in the United States of America by Cherry Lake Publishing
Ann Arbor, Michigan
www.cherrylakepublishing.com

Reading Adviser: Marla Conn, ReadAbility, Inc.
Book Designer: Melinda Millward

Photo Credits: © William Perugini/Shutterstock.com, back cover, 4; © monkeybusinessimages/Thinkstock.com, back cover, 4; © Peter Znoar/Shutterstock Images, cover, 1; © bo1982/iStock.com, 6; © Marcel Derweduwen/Shutterstock Images, 6; © Blulz60/iStock.com, 7; © Pressmaster/Shutterstock Images, 7; © Ken Durden / Shutterstock.com, 8; © Filipe Frazao/Shutterstock Images, 8; © Csehak Szabolcs/Shutterstock Images, 9; © Ron Ellis / Shutterstock.com, 9; © RyFlip/Shutterstock Images, 10; © Kiselev Andrey Valerevich/Shutterstock Images, 10; © Martin Novak/Shutterstock Images, 11; © SpeedKingz/Shutterstock Images, 11; © Rich Legg/iStock.com, 12; © Alan Bailey/Shutterstock Images, 12; © David_Ahn/iStock.com, 13; © jcjgphotography/Shutterstock Images, 13; © gradyreese/iStock.com, 14; © Monkey Business Images/Shutterstock Images, 14; © quavando/iStock.com, 15; © LuckyImages/Shutterstock Images, 15; © IM_photo/Shutterstock Images, 16; © Willyam Bradberry/Shutterstock Images, 16, 31; © Snap2Art / Shutterstock.com, 17; © Phillip Rubino / Shutterstock.com, 17; © Michael Woodruff / Shutterstock.com, 18; © Sergey Novikov/Shutterstock Images, 18; © Afby71 | Dreamstime.com - Skateboarder Photo, 19; © jason merideth/Shutterstock Images, 19; © SergeyIT/Shutterstock Images, 20; © MarclSchauer/Shutterstock Images, 20; © Madlen/Shutterstock Images, 21; © photka/Shutterstock Images, 21; © Indigo Fish/Shutterstock Images, 22; © Jaimie Duplass/Shutterstock Images, 22; © BrianWancho/Shutterstock Images, 23; © Halay Alex/Shutterstock Images, 23; © Syda Productions/Shutterstock Images, 24; © Luis Santos / Shutterstock.com, 24; © bikeriderlondon/Shutterstock Images, 25; © BlueSkyImage/Shutterstock Images, 25; © luanateutzi/Shutterstock Images, 26; © xmee/Shutterstock Images, 26; © Ryan Jorgensen – Jorgo/Shutterstock Images, 27; © Pop Paul-Catalin/Shutterstock Images, 27; © Christophe Michot / Shutterstock.com, 28; © Stefan Pircher/Shutterstock Images, 28; © Matt Berger/Shutterstock Images, 29; © My Good Images/Shutterstock Images, 29; © isitsharp/iStock.com, 30; © Eugene Onischenko/Shutterstock Images, 30; © Soloviova Liudmyla/Shutterstock Images, 31

Graphic Element Credits: © Silhouette Lover/Shutterstock Images, back cover, multiple interior pages; © Arevik/Shutterstock Images, back cover, multiple interior pages; © tukkki/Shutterstock Images, multiple interior pages; © paprika/Shutterstock Images, 24

45th Parallel Press is an imprint of Cherry Lake Publishing.

CIP data has been filed and is available at catalog.loc.gov.

Printed in the United States of America
Corporate Graphics

Table of Contents

Hey! Welcome to the Best Quiz Ever series. This is a book. Duh. But it's also a pretty awesome quiz. Don't worry. It's not about math. Or history. Or anything you might get graded on. Snooze.

This is a quiz all about YOU.

To Take the Best Quiz Ever:

Answer honestly!
Keep track of your answers. But don't write in the book!
(Hint: Make a copy of this handy chart.)
Don't see the answer you want? Pick the closest one.
Take it alone. Take it with friends!
Have fun! Obviously.

Question 1 _____   Question 7 _____

Question 2 _____   Question 8 _____

Question 3 _____   Question 9 _____

Question 4 _____   Question 10 _____

Question 5 _____   Question 11 _____

Question 6 _____   Question 12 _____

To get a copy of this activity, visit
www.cherrylakepublishing.com/activities.

Your favorite thing in gym class is:

A. capture the flag

B. Running the mile

C. Personal fitness challenge

D. Dodgeball

Did you know?
The world's largest dodgeball game had more than 6,000 people playing.

Pick a sporting event:

A. Super Bowl

B. World Cup

C. Olympics

D. Heavyweight Boxing **Championship**

Did you know?
The New England Patriots won
Super Bowl XLIX in 2015.

At first, people think you are:

A. Friendly

B. Cool

C. Aloof

D. Annoyed

Did you know?
Aloof means quiet and distant.

The inside of your locker is covered with:

A. Tons of pictures

B. A mirror

HOMEWORK

1. MATH
2. SCIENCE
3. ENGLISH
4.

C. A homework chart

D. Magazine ads

Did you know?

People have been using mirrors
since **prehistoric** times.

You have a day off from school. You:

A. Hang out with friends

B. Hope someone will take me to the mall

C. Go to the movies

D. Play outside

Did you know?

The movie Avatar made more than $2.8 billion.

The best way to get around is by:

A. Yacht

B. Private jet

C. Ducati

D. Off-road Jeep

Did you know?

The **yacht** Serene costs $5 million to rent for a week. It comes with two **helicopter** pads and a submarine.

Your X Games event would be:

A. Snowboard Cross

B. Mountain Bike Slopestyle

C. Skateboard Big Air

D. Snocross

Did you know?
Snocross is racing snowmobiles on
a track of jumps and **obstacles**.

Question 8

The best season is:

A. Summer

B. Spring

C. Fall

D. Winter

Did you know?

In 1977, Buffalo, New York, got 199.4 inches (5 meters) of snow. That's 16 feet of snow!

It's Winter Fest Dance! The most embarrassing thing would be:

A. Going alone

B. Wearing a lame outfit

C. Being there at all

D. My mom dropping me off

Did you know?
If you're "going stag" to a dance, it means you're going alone.

How did you find your favorite band?

A. The radio

B. An indie music blog

C. A friend

D. My dad

Did you know?
Pandora and Spotify are two of
the most popular radio apps.

On a scale of 1 to 10, getting punched in the face would be a:

A. 4 (I can handle it)

B. 7 (Ouch!)

C. 9 ($#@*!)

D. 2 (NBD)

Did you know?

Some scientists claim that swearing when you get hurt actually lowers the amount of pain you feel.

You would rather:

A. BASE jump

B. Cage dive

C. Climb Mount Everest

D. Go to Antarctica

Did you know?
Cage diving is being lowered into the sea in a protective cage. People can see sharks up close this way.

You're done! Now you tally your score. Add up your As, Bs, Cs, and Ds. What letter do you have the most of? BTW, if you have a tie, you're a little bit of both.

As: Football

You are Big Man on Campus. You're in a ton of clubs and sports. And you know everyone at school. Even the office ladies. You're determined. You have what it takes to tackle the other team. You aren't afraid of taking a big hit. Plus, you would love to be a Football Star. The bright lights. ESPN. Move over, Tom Brady.

Bs: Soccer

You know about trends before everyone. Your playlist is full of music your classmates have never heard of. You hang with a different sort of crowd. And you value loyalty in your friends. You'll for sure take the dive if you need to. And your friends would do the same. You're going to be a soccer pro! Start practicing that fancy footwork!

Cs: Swimming

You still don't love the idea of being on a team. You work best alone. You have a core group of great friends. But you also like being alone. You are very determined. And nothing can throw you off once you've set your mind to something. Don't feel comfortable being in a swimsuit in public? You should start getting used to the idea now. You're the next Michael Phelps!

Ds: Hockey

You get fired up over sports. REALLY fired up. You are crazy about your teams. In fact, you can get fired up about most things. Like that homework project. Or having to babysit. Again. You should definitely play hockey. Racing down the ice on fast skates sounds awesome. Throwing some well-padded checks sounds pretty sweet, too.

Glossary

capture (KAP-chur) to take and hold

championship (CHAM-pee-uhn-ship) final game of a series

helicopter (HEL-i-kahp-tur) an aircraft with large, spinning blades on top and no wings

obstacle (AHB-stuh-kuhl) something that makes it difficult to make progress

prehistoric (pree-hi-STOR-ik) belonging to a time before history was recorded in writing

yacht (yaht) a large boat used for fun

Index